Easy Spanish Phrases

Easy Spanish Phrase Book
New Edition

Over 700 Realistic Phrases for Everyday Use

First published in the United Kingdom 2020

Copyright 2020 @ by World Language Institute Spain

Midealuck Publishing Ltd.

ISBN 978-1-7392491-9-9

License Notice
This document is geared towards providing exact and reliable information regarding the topic and issue covered. In no way is it legal to reproduce, duplicate, or transmit any part of this document in either electronic means or in printed format. Recording of this publication is strictly prohibited and any storage of this document is not allowed unless with written permission from the publisher.

All Rights Reserved.
The information provided herein is stated to be truthful and consistent, in that any liability, in terms of inattention or otherwise, by any usage or abuse of any policies, processes, or directions contained within is the solitary and utter responsibility of the recipient reader. Under no circumstances will any legal responsibility or blame be held against the publisher for any reparation, damages, or monetary loss due to the information herein, either directly or indirectly. The information herein is offered for informational purposes solely and is universal as so. The presentation of the information is without contract or any type of guarantee assurance.

Chapters

Chapter 1 Learning the Structure & Basics of Spanish
Chapter 2 The Spanish Alphabet, Pronunciation, Syllabication, Stress & Rules for Capitalization
Chapter 3 Syllabication & Consonant
Chapter 4 Spanish Vowels & Rules of Stress
Chapter 5 Capitalization & Numbers
Chapter 6 Telling Time & Date in Spanish
Chapter 7 The First Steps of Learning the Language

Chapter 8 **Greetings & How to Address Spanish Speaking People**
Chapter 9 **Phrases for Formal & Informal Introductions**
Chapter 10 **Polite Expressions**
Chapter 11 **Phrases for Friends & Family**
Chapter 12 **Common Everyday Spanish**
Chapter 13 **Travel Phrases**
Chapter 14 **Restaurant & Eating Out**
Chapter 15 **Shopping & Renting**
Chapter 16 **Asking Directions**
Chapter 17 **Driving & Parking**
Chapter 18 **Transportation**
Chapter 19 **Medical Issues & Emergencies**
Chapter 20 **Banking Phrases & Terms**
Chapter 21 **Cleaning & Housekeeping**
Chapter 22 **Christmas Phrases & Expressions**
Chapter 23 **Guests & Invitations**
Chapter 24 **Insurance – Phrases & Terms**
Chapter 25 **Real Estate – Phrases & Terms**
Chapter 26 **Illness & Wellness**
Chapter 27 **Sports**
Chapter 28 **University & Education**
Chapter 29 **Computer & Social Media**
Chapter 30 **Airport & Flights**

Chapter 31 **Car Problems**
Chapter 32 **Spanish Foods**
Chapter 33 **Business & Negotiations**
Chapter 34 **Arts**
Chapter 35 **Entertainment & Recreation**
Chapter 36 **Crime & Help**
Chapter 37 **Taxi & Renting a Car**
Chapter 38 **General Repairs**
Chapter 39 **Going to Church**
Chapter 40 **Seasons, Festivals & Public Holidays**
Chapter 41 **Public Holidays**
Chapter 42 **Trivial Conversation**
Chapter 43 **Signs & Notices**
Chapter 44 **Legal Terms & Words**

Chapter 1

Learning the Structure & Basics of Spanish

The World Language Institute Spain wants to thank you for buying this book and extends a warm welcome to all readers.

This phrasebook contains proven and realistic phrases for everyday-use as well as lessons on the structure and basics of the language.

The first chapters explain the basics of the language and contain proven steps on how to learn Spanish in a reasonable short time and to a proper level.

We have prepared over 700 phrases for those with no or very little knowledge and who want to advance their language skills in the shortest time possible.

This book aims to provide a compact resource learning guide that includes essential phrases and terms for most situations.

Chapter 2

The Spanish Alphabet, Pronunciation, Syllabication, Stress & Rules for Capitalization

The Spanish Alphabet

Even though the pronunciation is different, Spanish language, uses basically the same Latin alphabet as used in English.

Correct pronunciation is key in Spanish as words are pronounced, spelled and written according to pronunciation.

The Spanish Alphabet & Pronunciation

Many Spanish letters are pronounced more or less the same way they are in English. But in some cases they are pronounced differently, and you must learn the correct pronunciation first before learning the phrases and expressions.

Diphtongs	English Sound
Ai	eye
Au	like ow in row
Ei	like in wet
Lo	like yo or yoyo
Oi	like oy in toy
Uo	like in woe
Iu	like in you
Ue	like wet
Ua	like wa in water

Letters	English Sound
a	like a in father
b,v	soft sound, between vowels
c	soft sound – the c in center or th thin
d	between vowels like th in the
e	like e in ley
f	like f forward
g	Before a,o,u: sound like goat
g	Before e and I: soft sound like Spanish j, in rare cases like English h (la jente) - the people
h	silent
i	Like i in machine

J	Throaty sound like h in ha!
K	like k in kilo
L	like l in call
Ll	pronounced as y
M	like m in Mike
N	like n in north
Ñ	like ny in canyon
O	like o in no
P	like p in posh
Q	like k, never as kw
R	thrilled sound like rr
T	like t in tone, without aspiration
U	like u in city of Tula
W	used for "borrowed" words
X	like x rex, in Latin America s.t. like the English sh
Y	like y in yes
Z	like center, or like th when used as vowel

Chapter 3

Syllabication & Consonant

Syllabication

Spanish syllables are almost always a consonant-vowel combination:

gato - ga-to : cat

casa - ca-sa :house

niña - ni-ña : young girl

sabana - sa-ba-na : blanket

Consonants

Usually, consonants are placed between two vowels and form a syllable, followed by a second vowel.

mesa - me-sa : table

oro - o-ro : gold

mano - ma-no : hand

Chapter 4

Spanish Vowels and Rules of Stress

Spanish Vowels

Spanish vowels are classified as either strong or weak vowels. The strong vowels are a, e, and the weak vowels are i and u. It's important to distinguish between strong and weak vowels as they play an important role in determining syllabication; one strong vowel in one syllable s therefore the norm.

Thus, two adjacent strong vowels must form two separate syllables. Two weak vowels may combine in one syllable to form one or more diphthongs. A strong vowel, however, may combine with a weak vowel into a single syllable.

Examples:

feo fe-o : ugly

creer cre-er : to believe

poeta po-e-ta : poet

reina rei-na : queen

Two consecutive consonants will usually form separate syllables.

siglo si-glo : century

cuando cuan-do : when

banco ban-co : bank

Some consonant combinations, however, are not separated and form a syllable together regardless of their placement: br, bl, cr, ch, cl, gl, dr, gr, fr, ll, fl, pl, pr, tr, qu, and rr.

broma bro-ma : joke
hecho he-cho : fact
bicicleta bi-ci-cle-ta : bicycle
clima cli-ma : climate
gloria glo-ria : glory
fruta fru-ta : fruit
llamar lla-mar : to call
frequente fre-quen-te : frequent
trabajo tra-ba-jo : job
aplicar a-pli-car : to apply
perro pe-rro : dog

Nevertheless, the consonant combinations such as rl, tl, sr, sl, and nr form separate syllables:
atlas at-las : atlas

perla per-la : pearl
isla is-la : isla
atlantico at-lan-ti-co : atlantic

When placing three consonants successively the first one usually forms part of a separate syllable.

entrada en-tra-da : entry

inglés in-glés : English

ombligo om-bli-go belly : button

panfleto pan-fle-to : pamphlet

constante con-stan-te : constant

Letter X is regarded as two consonants:

exámen ek-sa-men : exam

Rules of Stress

Spanish uses only one type of accent mark, the acute accent. It is used to indicate stress on a syllable. While Spanish words are generally stressed on one syllable, the stress is not always explicit or marked with an acute accent. In order to pronounce Spanish words accurately, you need to familiarize yourself with the rules on stress.

nación : nation

día : day

pájaro : bird

When there's no accent mark stress is usually determined by applying those simple rules:

Words ending in n, s, or a vowel receive the stress on the penultimate syllable. Thus:

e xa men : exam

lu nes : Monday

calce ti nes : socks

ca sa : house

When the word ends in a consonant other than n or s, the final syllable gets the stress.

ani mal : animal

pa red : wall

co mer : to eat

ciu dad : city

An accent mark is required when a syllable has to be stressed elsewhere. For instance, "el examen" ends in "n" and receives the accent on the penultimate syllable. When it forms the plural, however, it becomes "los exámenes". Take note that the stress falls on the same letter in singular and plural forms. The plural form, however, requires an explicit stress because the stress falls on a syllable other than the penultimate syllable.

When an unaccented weak vowel and a strong vowel are placed adjacent to each other to form a syllable, the strong vowel "receives" the stress.

pu e de : can

pe ru a no : Peruvian

An accented weak vowel placed beside a strong vowel forms a separate syllable.

biología bio-lo-gí-a : biology

policía po-li-cí-a :   police

The accent mark is also used to distinguish between homonyms and monosyllabic words. In such cases, the presence of the written accent will have no impact on pronunciation.

Examples:

mí (me) : mi (my) tú (you) : tu (your)
él (he) : el (the) sí (yes) : si (if)
sé (I know, be) : se (himself, herself) dé (give) : de (of, from)
más (more, most) : mas (but) té (tea) : te (you, yourself)

The written accent is likewise placed on interrogative words when they are used to ask questions:

¿Quién? : Who?

¿Cuál? : Which? ¿Dónde? : Where? ¿Qué? : What?/Which? ¿Cómo? : How?

¿Por qué? : Why? ¿Cuándo? : When? ¿Cuánto? : How many/much?

Accents are used to distinguish masculine and feminine demonstrative pronouns

éste, ésta : (this) éstos, éstas : (these) ése, ésa : (that) ésos, ésas : (those)

aquél, aquélla : (that over there) aquéllos, aquéllas : (those over there)

Chapter 5

Capitalization & Numbers

Spanish uses less capitalization than English. Capitalization is required in the following situations:

To start a sentence with proper nouns with shortened personal titles such as Sr., Dr., etc.

Capitalization is not required in these instances:

months (enero, febrero) days (jueves, viernes)

languages (francés, alemán, inglés)

Numbers

Spanish numbers are relatively easy to learn. First, you will have to memorize numbers zero to nineteen as these are unique numbers. In addition, you'll use these numbers as you progress to the bigger ones. The next step is to memorize the names for tens.

Take note that with numbers 21 to 29, you'll connect veinte and the Spanish words for one to nine by first changing the final 'e' to 'i'. Thus, twenty-one is veintiuno in Spanish. To form the rest of the tens digits starting with 30, you'll have to use the conjunction "y" (and). Thus, thirty-one becomes treinta y uno, forty-one becomes cuarenta y uno, etc.

Like most European languages, Spanish has inverse uses for the period and comma. You have to learn to use the comma to separate the whole numbers from the decimal numbers and the period to separate the numbers by hundreds. For example, the number 29,256,712.42 would be written in Spanish as 29.256.712,42.

The number uno (one) is variable and changes to "un" when it modifies a masculine noun and to "una" when it is used before a feminine noun.

Examples: un coche one car una casa one house
cincuenta y un hombres 51 men treinta y una casas 31 houses

The number ciento (100) takes the shortened form "cien" when used to describe a noun, when standing on its own, or when spoken. The "longer" form ciento is formed to express larger numbers other than mil.

Examples:

cien casas : 100 houses cien hombres : 100 men

cien mil casas : 100,000 houses ciento tres boligrafos : 103 pens

Cardinal Numbers

0 cero say-ro
1 uno oo-no
2 dos doss
3 tres trace
4 cuatro kwat-ro
5 cinco sink-o
6 seis saze
7 siete see-yet-eh
8 ocho och-o
9 nueve new-eh-veh
10 diez dee-ace
11 once ohn-say
12 doce dos-say
13 trece treh-seh
14 catorce ca-TOR-say
15 quince KEEN-say
16 dieciséis dee-AY-see-saze
17 diecisiete dee-AY-see-see-AY-tay
18 dieciocho dee-AY-see-och-o
19 diecinueve dee-AY-see-new-EH-veh
20 veinte Veh-een-tee
21 veintiuno Veh-een-tee-oo-no
22 veintidos Vehn-een-tee-DOS
23 ventitres Vehn-enn-tee-TRACE
24 venticuatro Vehn-een-tee-KWAT-ro
25 venticinco Vehn-een-tee-SINK-o
26 ventiseis Vehn-een-tee-saze
27 ventisiete Vehn-een-tee-say-tay
28 ventiocho Vehn-een-tee-OCHo
29 ventinueve Vehn-een-tee-new-EH-veh

30 treinta treh-een-tah
40 cuarenta kwar-EN-tah
50 cincuenta sink-KWEN-tah
60 sesenta seh-SEHN-tah
70 setenta seh-TEHN-tah
80 ochenta och-EHN-tah
90 noventa no-VEHN-tah
100 cien see-EHN

Ordinal numbers

first - primero
second - segundo
third - tecéro
fourth - cuatro
fifth - quinto
sixth - sexton
seventh - septimo
eight - octavo
ninth - noveno
tenth - decimo
11th - undécimo
12th - duodécimo
13th - decimotercero
14th - decimocuarto
15th - decimoquinto
16th - decimosexto
17th - decimoseptimo
18th - decimoctavo
19th - decimonoveno
20th - vigésimo

Ordinal numbers 21st-99th

The rest of the ordinal numbers below 100 are fairly simple. Write out each successive ordinal number as a separate word.

21st - vigésimo + primero = vigésimo primero

36th - trigésimo + sexto = trigésimo sexto

99th - nonagésimo + noveno = nonagésimo noveno

Ordinal numbers past 100

200th ducentésimo

300th tricentésimo

400th cuadringentésimo

500th quingentésimo

600th sexcentésimo

700th septingentésimo

800th octingentésimo

900th noningentésimo milésimo

Chapter 6

Telling Time & Date in Spanish

To ask what time is it in Spanish, you'll say: ¿Qué hora es?

Spain uses the twenty-four-hour format, just like other European countries, which in the US is also known as scientific or military time.

In Spanish you use only the singular feminine article "la" and the verb -es- to express time. At one o'clock. To express time for other hours, you only use the plural definite article -las- and the verb -son-. The verbs "es" and "son" are verb forms of "ser"(to be).

To tell time when the clock is at the exact hour:

Es la una. It's one o'clock.

Son las seis. It's six o'clock.

Son las diez. It's ten o'clock.

When time is past the hour you can express the minutes with the conjunction "y" : (and).

Examples: 8:20 Son las ocho y veinte. - It is twenty minutes past eight o'clock.

1:05 Es la una y cinco. - It is five minutes past one.

When time is a few minutes before an approaching hour, you can use the word "menos" to express the number of minutes left to complete the next hour.

Examples: 8:45 Son las nueve menos quince. - It's 15 minutes before nine o'clock. 9:48

Son las diez menos doze. - It's 12 minutes before ten o'clock.

You can use the word "media" (half) to express the half hour and and "cuarto" (quarter) to express quarter of an hour.

3:30 Son las dos y media : It's half past three.

1:30 Es la una y media : It's half past one.

3:15 Son las tres y cuarto : It's a quarter past three.

2:45 Son las doz menos cuarto : It's a quarter before three.

21:15 Son las veintiuno y cuarto : It's a quarter past 9 o'clock pm.

The time expressions a.m. and p.m. are not used in Spanish. You will instead descrcibe the part of day by adding "de la mañana", "de la tarde", and "de la noche" in the morning, afternoon, and evening respectively.

Examples: Son las cuatro y media de la mañana. It's half past four in the morning. Son las tcuatro de la tarde. It's four o'clock in the afternoon. Son las once de la noche. It's eleven o'clock in the evening.

Telling the Date in Spanish

To ask for the date, you can say:

¿Qué día es hoy? What day is today?

¿Cuál es la fecha de hoy? What is the date today? To tell the date use this pattern: *el*+number+*de*+month+*de*+year

For the first day of the month, use the ordinal number primero.

For the rest of the days use a cardinal number.

Examples:

May 13, 2019 el trece de mayo de 2019.

January 11, 2019 el once de enero de 2019.

August 1, 2019 el primero de agosto de 2019.

To express the current date, you can say:

Hoy es el doce de abril de 2019. Today is April 12, 20....

Hoy es lunes, el 19 de abril de 2019. Today is Monday, the 19th day of April, 2019.

Take note that in Spanish, the day is expressed before the month and year. This holds true when you tell the date in figures. Hence, while you would write 12/15/2017 to express December 15, 2017 in English, it will be written as 15/12/2015 in Spanish.

The year is expressed like a regular number in Spanish. For instance, to say that the year is 2017, you'll say: dos mil dieciséis.

Chapter 7

First Steps – Learning First Words and Essay Expressions

Greeting people is a basic way to show courtesy and start or nurture good relationships. In this chapter, you will learn common Spanish greetings and expressions that you can use to meet new people, greet friends, and express yourself in different situations.

Chapter 8

Greetings & How to Address Spaniards

There are two ways of addressing people in Spanish: the familiar and the formal. To address people with whom you have a relationship on a first name basis, you will use the familiar way. To address people who are older, your superior, and new acquaintances, you will use the formal way.

To greet people formally, you will use the usted/ustedes (Ud. for usted, and Uds. for ustedes) form of the verb. You may also address people with titles such as señor or "señora" or by their profession.

Here are common formal greetings:

¿Cómo está usted señor? How are you, mister?

¿Cómo le va? How are you?

¿Que tal? How is it going?

Here are common informal greetings:

¡Hola! Hello!

Hola, buenas tardes. Hello, good afternoon.

¿Cómo estás? How are you? ¿Cómo te va? How's it going?

¿Qué hay? What's up? ¿Qué tal? How are things?

To say goodbye, you can use an applicable phrase from this list:

Adiós. Goodbye.

Nos vemos. We'll see each other.

Hasta luego. See you later. Hasta pronto. See you soon.

Hasta muy pronto. See you very soon.

Hasta ahora. See you in a minute.

Hasta mañana. Until tomorrow.

The famous phrase, Hasta la vista. Until we see each other - is actually a form of Mexican slang, and is not official Spanish, and seen as lack of education in many Spanish speaking countries.

Hasta el lunes. See you on Monday.

Cuidate. Take care.

Chapter 9

Phrases for Formal & informal introductions

In general, you will use the formal way when meeting people for the first time.

To ask for someone's name who is unknown to you (formal), you will say:
¿Cómo se llama usted? What's your name? KOH-moh say YAHM-ah oo-STED

The informal way may be appropriate when:

you know the person

meeting a child or a person who is about your age

you are in a group or meeting that is informal in nature (f.e. a party)

¿Cómo te llamas? What's your name? KOH-mo tay YAHM-ahss

To introduce yourself, you can say: My name is _____.
Me llamo _____. may YAHM-oh

State your name I am
_____. **Soy** _____.

My name is (first and last name)_____.
Mi nombre es _____. may NOM-bre

You can use any of these phrases to express your pleasure at the meeting:

¡Muchísimo gusto!
I'm very pleased to meet you!

¡Mucho gusto!
Nice to meet you!

Es un gusto conocerle
It's a pleasure to meet you.

To introduce people to each other, you can say:

Este es mi amigo John.
This is my friend John.

John, esta es mi hermana Maria.
John, this is my sister Maria.

Chapter 10

Polite Expressions

These polite expressions will help you make a good impression:

Thank you very much!
¡Muchas gracias!

It's okay
Esta bien

No, thanks
No, gracias

You are welcome
De nada

Excuse me
Perdóneme/Discúlpeme"/Desculpa

Sorry
Perdón

I am very sorry
Lo siento mucho

You are very kind
Eres muy amable

Chapter 11

Phrases for Greeting Friends & Family

What's your name?
¿Cómo te llamas? ¿Cómo se llama usted?

My name is .....
Me llamo .....

How are you? -
¿Cómo estás? ¿Cómo está?

Very well, thank you
Muy bien, gracias

Good day, good morning
Buenos días

Good afternoon
Buenas tardes

Good night
Buenas noches

What's going on?
¿Que pasa?

Nice to meet you -
Encantado / Con mucho gusto

May I introduce you my sister
Te presento mi Hermana

Do you have siblings?
Tienes/Tiene hermanos

This is my brother
Es mi hermano

This is my sister
Es mi hermana

This is my uncle
Es mi tío

This is my aunt
Es mi tía

This is my grandmother
Es mi abuela

This is my grandfather
Es mi abuelo

I have a son / I have a daughter
Tengo un hijo / Tengo una hija

I am waiting for my mother
Espero a mi madre

When can we meet?
Cuando podemos encontrar?

Where can we meet
Donde podemos encontrar?

This person is part of my family
Este persona es parte de mi familia

I have a boyfriend / a girlfriend
Tengo un novio / una novia

I invite you to meet my family
Te envito que conozcas mi familia

Come to my house
Ven a mi casa

Chapter 12

Common Everyday Spanish Phrases

I want, I don't want
Yo quiero, yo no quiero

I would like..
Me gustaría ..

Where is..?
¿Dónde está..?

How much does it cost?
¿Cuánto cuesta?

What time is it?
Qué hora es?

Do you have...?
¿Tiene...?

I have / I don't have...
Yo tengo, yo no tengo...

I understand / I don't understand
Yo entiendo, yo no entiendo

Do you understand?
¿Entiende?

Chapter 13

Travel Phrases

I am looking for a hotel
Estoy buscando a un hotel

I want a room with private bathroom
Quiero una habitación con baño privado

Do you have a cheaper room?
¿Tiene una habitación más barata?

Can you call me a taxi, please?
¿Me puede llamar a un taxi, por favor?

Bring me to the airport!
al aeropuerto!

When is the next flight to..?
¿Cuándo es el próximo vuelo a..?

At what time does the flight from...arrive?
¿A qué hora llega el vuelo de ... ?

Where is the exchange?
¿Dónde está una casa de cambio?

Where is the bank?
¿Dónde está el banco?

Where is the bus station?
¿Donde esta la estación del bus

Where can I buy a ticket to...?
¿Dónde puedo comprar un boleto/tickete a..?

I pay the ticket with my credit card
Yo pago el billtete con mi tarjeta de credito

Chapter 14

Restaurant & Eating Out Phrases

I like to order a coffee
Me gusta pedir un café

Can I have the menu please?
¿Puedo tener el menú favor?

We would like to reserve a table
Nos gustaría reservar una mesa

Do you have vegetarian meals?
¿Tiene comidas vegetariano?

I like to have my steak medium rare
Me gustaría tener mi carne poco hecho

The food is unacceptable
La comida es inaceptable

Bring me something else
Tráeme algo diferente

I would like to order a glass of white wine
Me gustaría pedir una copa de vino blanco

The bill / check please
La cuenta por favor

The tip is not included
La propina no está incluido

Chapter 15

Shopping and Renting

We are looking for a good souvenir
Estamos buscando un buen recuerdo

Do you have a larger size? This is too small -
¿Tiene un tamaño mas grande? Esto es demasiado pequeña

Esta camiseta es demasiada cara
This shirt is too expensive

Is the price negotiable?
¿Es negociable el precio?

I only want to buy fresh ingredients
Yo sólo quiero comprar ingredientes frescos

How much is the weekly rent?
¿Cuánto cuesta el alquiler semanal?

Do we have to pay a deposit?
¿Hay que pagar un depósito?

We are looking for a furnished room
Estamos buscando una habitación amueblada

We like to rent this room by the month
Nos gustaría alquilar esta habitación por el mes

When do I get my money back?
¿Cuándo recibo mi dinero?

The house needs to be cleaned
La casa necesita limpieza

Chapter 16

Asking Directions

Where is..?
Dónde está.. ?

Can you tell me the way to..?
Me puedes decir el camino de ?

Can you show me on the map?
¿Me puede mostrar en el mapa?

Can you walk?
¿Puede caminar?

Where are the toilets?
¿Dónde están los aseos / servicios?

Is it near?
¿Está cerca?

Is it far?
¿Está lejos?

Is there a bus that goes there?
¿Hay un bús que va allí?

Where does this road go to?
¿A dónde va este camino?

Which direction?
¿Qué dirección?

I am looking for the next exit
Estoy buscando la siguiente salida

Is this the street to...?
¿Se va por aqui a..?

Where can I find the....? -
¿Donde puedo encontrar ...?

Left
A la izquierda

Right
A la derecha

Turn right
Gira a la derecha

On the corner
En la esquina

Opposite the gas / petrol station
Frente a la gaseolera

You have to go back
Tiene que dar la vuelta

Keep going straight ahead
Siga todo recto

Take the road for...
Coja la carretera de...

Under the bridge
Bajo el Puente

It's at the crossroads
Esta en la cruze

You go as far as..
Vaya hasta..

It's next to the supermarket
Esta junto al supermercado

Cross the street
Crucear la calle

On the second floor
En el siguiente piso

The supermarket is in front of the church.
El supermercado esta a frente de iglesia.

The embassy is across the main street.
La embajada esta a otro lado de avenida principal.

The hospital is around the corner
La clínica esta la vuelta de la esquina.

About how long will that take?
¿Acerca de cuánto tiempo se tardará?

You go straight, and then you turn left.
Bas directamente y luego gire a la izquierda.

Chapter 17

Driving & Parking Phrases

Is the traffic heavy?
Hay mucho trafico?

Is there a different way to the airport?
¿Hay una manera diferente al aeropuerto?

What is causing this traffic jam?
¿Qué está causando este tráfico jam?

When will the road be clear?
¿Cuándo estará clara la carretera?

What is the speed limit?
¿Cuál es el límite de velocidad?

Is there a toll on this motorway?
¿Hay un peaje de esta autopista?

Can you clean the windscreen?
¿Puede limpiar el parabrisas?

We got lost!
¡Estamos perdidos!

Slow the car down
frenar el coche

Can you drive faster?
¿Puede conducir más rápido?

I need to get out here
Tengo que salir de aquí

We are looking for a gas / petrol station
Estamos buscando de una gaseolera

Can I park here?
¿Puedo aparcar aquí?

Where is the nearest parking garage?
¿Dónde está el garaje más cercano?

How long can I stay here?
¿Cuánto tiempo me puedo quedar aquí?

Where do I pay?
¿Dónde pagar?

Fill the tank please
Llena el tanke por favor

This is my drivers license
Este es mi licencia de conducir

Chapter 18

Transportation Phrases

Where is the bus stop? -
¿Dónde dónde está la parada de autobus?

Where is the train station? -
¿Donde esta la estacion de trenes?

Where is the ticket machine? -
¿Dónde está la máquina de billetes?

Is that within walking distance? -
¿Se puede ir andando?

Where do I transfer? -
¿Dónde puedo transferir?

How much luggage may I bring? –
¿Cuánto equipaje puedo llevar?

At what gate will I find the airplane? -
¿A qué puerta voy a encontrar el avión?

The flight has been delayed -
El vuelo se ha retrasado.

Does this bus stop in Granada too? -
¿Se para este bus tambien en Granada?

Is there a stopover?
¿Hay una escala?

Is there public transportation?
¿Hay transporte público?

When do we arrive?
¿Cuándo llegamos?

What is the name of the next station?
Como se llama la proxima estacion?

Is the next stop the bus station?
Donde esta la estacion de buses?

Chapter 19

Medical Issues & Emergencies

Where is the next hospital?
¿Dónde está la próxima clínica?

Our insurance in the US will pay for this
Nuestro seguro en los Estado Unidos pagará por este

My wife needs surgery
Mi esposa necesita una cirugía

I need to have my tooth fixed
Necesito mi diente roto reparado

Do you have strong painkillers?
Usted tiene analgésicos fuertes?

I am allergic against... (fish)
Soy alérgico a.... (marisco)

I had an accident, please send an ambulance
He tenido un accidente, por favor, envíe una ambulancia

I need a remedy against headache
Necesito un remedio contra el dolor de cabeza

I cut myself, do you have a bandage?
Me corto, tienes un vendaje?

Can you send a doctor to my house?
¿Se puede enviar un doctor a mi casa?

Chapter 20

Banking Phrases & Terms

I need an ATM
Necesito un cajero

Do they change dollar?
¿Se cambian dolares?

I'd like to open a checking account
Me gustaría abrir una cuenta de cheques

I like to open a savings account.
Me gustaría abrir una cuenta de ahorros

What documents do I need to open a bank account?
¿Que documentos necesito para abrir una cuenta bancaria?

The ATM machine did not dispense notes
El cajero automático no dispensó billetes

I want to apply for a personal credit
Quiero solicitar un crédito personal

I want to cash a cheque
Quiero cobrar un cheque

I need cash money from my account
Necesito dinero en efectivo de mi cuenta.

Chapter 21

Phrases for House Cleaning

We need a charlady
Necesitamos una mujer de limpieza (S.A muchacha)

Please clean the corners too
Por favor tambien limpia las escinas

Clean the carpet with a vacuum cleaner
Limpia la alfombra con la aspiradora

Please clean the windows
Por favor limpia las ventanas

Put the bottles into the refrigerator
Guarda los botellas en la nevera

You need to make your bed
Lo que necesita para hacer su cama

Can you water the plants please?
¿Puede por favor regar las plantas?

Turn down the heating
Baja la calefacción

Screw a new light bulb into the lamp
Atornillar una nueva bombilla en la lámpara

You have to mob the floor
Tienes que trapear el piso

Bring the trash outside
Llevar la basura fuera

Please empty the buckets
Por favor, vaciar los cubos

Carry the cases into the basement
Llevar a los casos en el sótano

Don't forget to clean the closets
No se olvide de limpiar los armarios

Fluff and shake the pillows
Pelusa y sacude las almohadas

Close the shutters
Cierre las persianas

Don't forget to lock the doors
No se olvide cerrar las puertas

Spray the rooms with insect spray
Pulveriza las habitaciones con repelente de insectos

Roll up the carpets
Enrolla las alfombras

The bathroom needs to be cleaned
El baño necesita ser limpiado

Polish the mirrors
Pulir los espejos

You are not allowed to make a break
No se le permite hacer una pausa

We pay you once a month
Le pagamos una vez al mes

Open all the windows
Abierta todo las ventanas

We appreciate your good work
Agradecemos su buen trabajo

Chapter 22

Christmas Phrases & Expressions

We are looking for a Christmas gift
Buscamos un regalo para Navidad

Where are the Christmas markets?
Dónde están los mercados de Navidad?

Can you wrap it up please?
¿Se puede envolverlo por favor?

They don't have Santa Claus in Spain
No hay santa claus en España

In some countries he's called papa noel
En algunos paises se llama papa noel

Christmas songs are important
Canciones de Navidad son importante

We are looking for a Christmas tree
Estamos buscando un árbol de navidad

We need help to decorate the Christmas tree
Necesitamos ayuda para decorar el árbol de Navidad

We are going to visit our family for Christmas
En navidad vamos a visitar a la familia

What do you have for Christmas dinner?
¿Qué hay para la cena de Navidad?

We only go to church at Christmas
Nosotros sólo vamos a la iglesia en Navidad

I have a Christmas gift for you
Tengo un regalo de Navidad para ti

Chapter 23

Guests and Invitations

Please lay the table for dinner
Por favor cubra la mesa por la cena

Would you please greet our guests?
¿Por favor saludar a los invitados?

Welcome to our house
Bienvenido a nuestra casa

You are most welcome
Ustedes son bienvenidos

We have prepared dinner for you
Hemos preparado la cena para usted

You can bring your family
Puede traer a su familia

Tonight we are expecting guests
Esta noche estamos invitados esperando

I have received an invitation
He recibido una invitación

We are part of your family
Somos parte de su familia

This is the key for the main entrance
Esta es la clave para la entrada principal

This is the key for your room
Esta es su llave para su habitación

Where can we leave our luggage?
¿Dónde podemos dejar nuestro equipaje?

I would like to invite you
Me gustaría invitarle

We have to cancel our reservation
Tenemos que cancelar nuestra reserva

We are organizing a barbecue evening
Estamos organizando una noche de barbacoa

We have a bathroom for men and for women
Tenemos un cuarto de baño para los hombres y para las mujeres

Do you have a guest house ?
¿Tiene una casa de huéspedes?

We prefer to sleep in a private room
Nosotros preferimos dormir en una habitación privada

We had a great time
Tuvimos un tiempo estupendo

There is no smoking in the room
No se puede fumar en la habitación

Can you please turn down the volume?
¿Puede por favor baje el volumen

Please take the trash outside
Por favor, tome la basura fuera

Please clean the room before you leave
Por favor, limpiar la habitación antes de salir

There is a cleaning fee before you leave
Hay una tarifa de limpieza antes de salir

Unfortunately you have damaged something
Desafortunadamente, usted ha dañado algo

Chapter 24

Insurance – Phrases & Terms

Do you have insurance?
¿Tienes seguro?

Is your car insured
¿Está asegurado su coche?

Do you have liability insurance?
Tienes seguro de responsabilidad civil?

We would like to insure the car
Nos gustaría asegurar el coche

I need a household insurance
Necesito un seguro de hogar

Let me get my insurance papers
Dejame tenerlo mis papeles de seguro

I have everything insured
Todo lo que he asegurado

We should file the police report
Debemos presentar un informe policial

We need to file a damage report
  Tenemos que presentar un informe de daños

Are they going raise our premiums?
  ¿Van a elevar nuestras primas?

We don't agree with your appraiser '
  No estamos de acuerdo con su tasador

I am the beneficiary
  Soy el beneficiario

Can we get a free quote?
  Podemos obtener un presupuesto gratuito ?

Where can I buy a car insurance
  ¿Dónde puedo comprar un seguro de coche

I just need liability insurance
  Sólo necesito un seguro de responsabilidad

We would like to insure our property
  Nos gustaría asegurar nuestra propiedad

Can we pay by annual installments?
  Se puede pagar en cuotas anuales?

What are the deductibles?
  Cuáles son los deducibles?

I need property insurance.
Necesito un seguro de propiedad

You have to submit underwriting
Usted tiene que someter a evaluación de riesgo

I want an accidental death insurance
un seguro de muerte accidental

Chapter 25

Real Estate – phrases & Terms

What kind of neighbors do you have?
¿Qué clase de vecinos tiene usted?

When was this house built?
¿Cuando se construyó esta casa?

How much is the property tax?
¿Cuánto es el impuesto a la propiedad?

How much are the annual running costs ?
¿Cuánto son los gastos anuales de funcionamiento?

We would like to view the house
Nos gustaría ver la casa

Are you the owner of this property?
¿Eres dueño de esta propiedad?

Is this house rented?
Se alquila esta casa?

Who is living in this house?
Quien esta viviendo en este casa?

Is there a community pool?
Hay piscina comunitaria?

How much is the administration fee?
¿Cuánto es la cuota de administración?

How many square meters has the land?
¿Cuántos metros cuadrados tiene la tierra?

How many square feet has this house?
¿Cuántos pies cuadrados tiene esta casa?

This house needs to be renovated
Esta casa necesita ser reformada

How many people are registered in the deed?
¿Cuántas personas están registrados en la escritura?

Do you have a floor plan?
¿Tiene un plan de piso?

Is this house owned by the bank?
¿Es esta casa propiedad del banco ?

We don't need a realtor
No necesitamos un agente inmobiliario

Who is paying the closing fees?
¿Quién paga los gastos de cierre?

Do you offer owner financing?
¿Ofrecen financiamiento del dueño?

Chapter 26

Illness & Wellness

I am sick
Estoy enfermo

I don't feel well
No me siento bien

I need an doctor who speaks English
Necesito a un doctor que hable inglés

I need a dentist
Necesito un dentista

It's an emergency
Es una emergencia

I need an appointment
Necesito una cita

My back hurts
Mi espalda duele

I have dislocated my shoulder
He dislocado el hombre

My throat bothers me
Mi garganta me molesta

I have pain in my chest
Tengo dolor en mi pecho

My stomach hurts
Mi dolor de estómago

My foot is inflamed
Mi pie se inflama

I broke my arm
Rompí mi brazo

I prefer natural product and natural healing
Prefiero productos naturales y curas naturales

I am infected with S.T.D.
Estoy contagiado de S.T.D.

I have diabetis
Tengo diabetes

I have liver problems
Tengo problemas de hígado

Is my disease serious?
¿Es mi enfermedad grave?

I have a terminal illness
Tengo una enfermedad terminal

It hurts in this part of the body
Me duele en esta porción del cuerpo

I need painkillers
Yo necesito analgésicos

I want to go to a spa
Quiero ir a un sauna

I need new glasses
Necesito nuevas gafas

I need a prescription for..
Necesito una receta para...

Where can I find a specialist for..?
¿Donde puedo encontrar un especialista para..?

I need medication for..
Necesito medicamentos para..

I need pills against..
Necesito pastillas contra..

I need a diagnostic
Es necesario un diagnóstico

Can you call a doctor?
¿Puede usted llamar a un doctor?

Can you call an ambulance?
¿Se puede llamar una ambulancia?

Can you drive me to the hospital?
¿Puede llevarme al hospital?

I am suffering under pain
Estoy sufriendo de dolor

I suffer from indigestion
Sufro de indigestión

I threw up
Vomité

I am dizzy
Estoy mareado

I cut myself
Yo corté

I need band aid
Necesito un parche

Where is the next pharmacy?
¿Dónde está la farmacia próxima?

Does the medicine cause side effects?
¿El medicamento causa efectos secundarios?

Chapter 27

Sport Terms & Phrases

We like soccer
Nos gusta el fútbol

When does the game start?
¿Cuándo comienza el partido?

Are you a fan of...?
¿Eres fan de...?

. Can we join the group?
¿Nosotros podemos participar en el grupo?

We like sports
Nos gusta el deporte

We would like to jog on the beach
Nos gustaria corer en la playa

Where can we rent a bycicle?
¿Donde podemos alquilar una bicicleta?

Does this place has a gym?
¿Este lugar tiene un gimnasio?

How much is membership?
¿Cuánto es miembro?

I need to make excercise to lose weight
Necesito hacer ejercicio para bajar de peso

I like to play tenis
Me gusta jugar tenis

I like to swim
Me gusta nadar

I am looking for a yoga group
Estoy buscando un grupo de yoga

I want to find a fitness instructor
Quiero encontrar un instructor de deportes

Can you help me to lift the weights?
Me puedes ayudar a levantar las pesas?

I want to do aerobics
Quiero hacer aerobic

I want to start slowly
Quiero empezar poco a poco

We are looking for a good diving spot
Estamos buscando un buen punto de buceo

Chapter 28

University and Education

Where can I register?
¿Donde puedo matricular?

When is semester break?
¿Cuándo son las vacaciones de semestre?

What is your principal area of study?
¿Cuál es su área principal de estudios?

When is the examen
¿Cuándo es el examen?

Let's to to the university!
Vamos a la universidad!

What is the campus policy?
¿Cuál es la política de la escuela?

How much is the tuition fee?
¿Cuánto es la cuota tución?

Does this college still have places available?
¿Todavia hay plazas en este universidad?

What are the undergraduate degree courses?
¿Cuáles son los cursos de licenciatura?

Does this university offer financial aid?
¿Esta universidad ofrece ayuda financiera?

What final degrees does this university offer?
¿Qué títulos se ofrece esta universidad?

What are the discipline's seminal papers?
¿Cuáles son los papeles seminales de la disciplina?

Is the food in the canteen free and edible?
¿Es la comida en la cantina libre y comestible?

Do I need to deliver a master's thesis?
¿Tengo que entregar una tesis de maestría?

I meet you in the auditorium
Me encuentro en el auditorio

This university has an entrance examination
Esta universidad tiene un examen de ingreso

Chapter 29

Computer and Social Media

Can I join your group?
¿Puedo unirme a tu grupo?

Is advertising allowed?
¿Se permite la publicidad?

I would like to participate
Me gustaría participar

What are the rules for this group?
¿Cuáles son las reglas de este grupo?

Please don't spam my account
Por favor no spam a mi cuenta

Can you help me to find an app in Spanish?
¿Me puedes ayudar a encontrar una aplicación en Español?

Can you help me to install a program?
¿Me puedes ayudar a instalar un programa?

I want to buy only original components
Quiero comprar solamente componentes originales

Does this item have proper cables?
¿Este artículo tiene cables adecuados?

The printer doesn't print
La impresora no imprime

Where can if buy printer cardridges?
¿donde puedo comprar cartuchas?

Is there a computer repair shop nearby?
¿Hay un servico technico de computadora cerca?

My tablet needs a new glass
Mi tablet necesita un nuevo vidrio

Can you give me an estimate?
¿Me puede dar un presupuesto?

Where can I download this?
¿Donde puedo descargar esto?

I want to return this product
Quiero regresar este producto

Chapter 30

Airport and Flights

What is our flight number?
¿Cuál es nuestro número de vuelo?

I have a reservation
Tengo una reserve

have only one suitcase
Tengo solo una maleta

I have only hand luggage
Tengo solo equipaje de mano

Can we take that into the cabin?
¿Podemos tomar dentro de la cabina?

I need a boarding pass
Can we take that into the cabin?

Where do I claim the luggage?
¿Dónde puedo reclamar el equipaje?

Where can we find gate number… ?
Dónde podemos encontrar puerta numero… ?

I need to change my ticket
Necesito cambiar mi billete

The airline changed our flight
La aerolínea cambió nuestro vuelo

I would like to have a window seat
Me gustaría tener un asiento de ventana

I would like to have an aisle seat
Me gustaría tener un asiento del pasillo

Can I get an upgrade?
¿Puedo obtener una actualización?

Do we have to go through security?
¿Tenemos que pasar por seguridad?

Where is the information desk?
¿Dónde está el mostrador de información?

This computer belongs to me
Este ordenador es mio

I have nothing to declare
No tengo nada que declarer

Do you know at what time are we arriving?
¿Sabes a que hora estamos llegando?

I would like to change my seat
Me gustaría cambiar mi asiento

Where do I claim my luggage?
¿Dónde reclamo mi equipaje?

Where is the arrival terminal?
¿Dónde está el terminal de llegados

Where is the terminal for departure?
¿Dónde está el terminal de salidas?

Our luggage has not arrived
Nuestro equipaje no ha llegado

Do you have a hotel voucher for us?
¿Usted tiene un bono de hotel para nosotros?

Where do I find the shuttle transfer to Terminal 1?
¿Dónde puedo encontrar el traslado a la Terminal 1?

Where do I find the car rental companies?
¿Dónde puedo encontrar los companias coches de aquilar?

Chapter 31

Car Problems – Phrases and Terms

We would like to rent a car
Nos gustaría alquilar un coche

We had an accident
Tuvimos un accidente

They have towed the car
Se han remolcado el coche

I need a tow truck
Nesecito - la grua / el carro de remolque

The car has a flat tire
El coche tiene una rueda pinchada

The car won't start
El coche no arranca

It is leaking oil
Gotea aceite

Can you recommend a garage?
¿Me puede recomendar un taller?

Can you fix it?
¿Puede usted arreglarlo?

How long does it take?
¿Cuánto tiempo tarda?

Where can I return the car?
¿Dónde puedo devolver el coche?

Chapter 32

Spanish Foods

What is your favorite food?
¿Cuál es tu comida favorita?

Can you please explain what that is?
¿Por favor, podría explicar lo que es?

It tastes very interesting
Tiene un sabor muy interesante

. This is very delicious
Esto es muy delicioso

We would like to order..
Nos gustaría ordenar...

Can you bring us a larger portion please?
¿Usted nos puede traer una porción más grande por favor?

What are the ingredients for this dish?
¿Cuáles son los ingredientes para este plato?

How do you make paella?
¿Como se hace Paella?

We like traditional food
Nos gusta la comida tradicional

What is a good Spanish diet meal?
¿Qué es una comida buena dieta española?

How many calories are in there?
¿Cuántas calorías se están allí?

What food do you recommend for weight loss?
¿Qué alimentos me recomiendan para bajar peso?

What typical Spanish dishes do you know?
¿Qué platos típicos españoles conoces?

What are typical ingredients used in Spain?
¿Qué ingredientes típicos se utilizan en España?

First you fry it than you bake it
Primero se fríe despues se cuece al horno

We prefer sweet flavors
Nos prefieren sabores dulces

We prefer earthy flavors
Nosotros preferimos sabores terrosos

How do you cook this dish?
¿Cómo cocinar este plato?

We would like to buy ham
Nos gustaría comprar jamón

Chapter 33

Phrases for Business & Negotiations

I need a receipt / bill
Necesito un recibo / una factura

I am interested
Estoy interesado

Thank's, but I am not interested
Gracias, pero no me interesa

I need to speak with the owner
Necesito hablar con el propietario

Is the price negociable?
¿Es el precio negociable?

This is my team
Este es mi equipo

Let's make a contract
Vamos a hacer un contrato

We would like to renegotiate
Nos gustaría renegociar

We like to order
We like to order

When can you deliver?
¿Cuándo puede entregar?

Who is paying customs?
¿Quien paga la aduana?

How much are the total costs?
¿Cuánto son los costes totales?

What is your best price?
¿Cuál es su mejor precio?

We want to cancel
Queremos cancelar

The price is too high
El precio es demasiado alto

Are taxes included?
¿Son impuestos incluidos?

How much is the commission?
¿Cuánto es la Comisión?

I need a non disclosure agreement
Necesito un acuerdo de no divulgación

How much taxes we have to pay?
¿Cuánto impuestos tenemos que pagar?

What are the delivery terms?
¿Cuáles son las condiciones de entrega?

Does this product has warranties?
¿Este producto tiene garantía?

Will you accept the order
Aceptará la orden

We want to make you an offer
Queremos hacerte una oferta

We will consider your offer
Consideramos su oferta

We have to reject your offer
Tenemos que rechazar su oferta

We pay after delivery
Pagamos después de la entrega

We pay into an escrow account
Pagamos a una cuenta de fideicomiso

Can I pay with a credit card?
¿Puedo pagar con tarjeta de crédito?

You have to fulfil the order
Tienes que cumplir la orden

Chapter 34

Arts

Where is the museum?
¿Dónde está el Museo?

This is very magnificent
Es muy magnífico

Who created all of this?
¿Quién creó todo esto?

They have a sense for beauty
Tienen un sentido para la belleza

We appreciate art
Apreciamos el arte

Can you change the design?
¿Se puede cambiar el diseño?

Who is the artist?
¿Quién es el artista?

This is a beautiful painting
Esta es una hermosa pintura

How old is it?
¿Cuántos años tiene?

Does it have a signature?
¿Tiene una firma?

What technique did the artist use?
¿Qué técnica utiliza el artista?

How do you call this artistic style?
¿Cómo se llama este estilo artístico?

How did you clean this artwork?
¿Como has limpiado este obra de arte?

We are only interested in authentic fine arts
Sólo estamos interesados en auténtico bellas artes

This item has only a personal value
Este artículo tiene sólo un valor personal

Is this antiquity original or a replica?
¿Es esta antigüedad original o una réplica?

Chapter 35

Entertainment and Recreation

Tonight we would like to go out
Esta noche queremos salir

Can we go to a concert?
Podemos ir a un concierto?

How much are the tickets?
Cuanto cuestan los boletos?

We will meet at the entrance
Nos encontramos en la entrada

What kind of movie do you like?
¿Qué tipo de película te gusta?

Did you like the movie?
¿Te gustó la película?

Can you recommend a good night club?
¿Me puede recomendar un buen antro / club?

Do you like dancing?
¿Te gusta bailar?

Shall we dance?
¿Bailamos?

This is fun!
Esto es divertido!

This is boring.
Esto es aburrido

Let's go someplace else
Vamos a otro lado

Do they have a botanical garden?
¿Tienen un jardín botánico?

Is there a public swimming pool?
¿Hay una piscina pública?

Is there an amusement park nearby?
Hay un parque de diversiones cerca

We would like to visit a spa
Nos gustaría visitar un spa

Where can I get a massage?
¿Dónde puedo conseguir un masaje?

Is the movie in original language?
¿Es la película en idioma original?

Chapter 36

Crime and Help Phrases

I need a doctor
Necesito un médico

I need help!
Necesito ayuda!

Call the police!
¡Llamar a la policía!

I am going to call the police
Voy a llamar a la policía

This is an emergency
Se trata de una emergencia

Stop the thief!
¡Alto al ladrón!

I am a witness
Soy un testigo

I have not seen anything
No he visto nada

I have been robbed
Me han robado

I have been attacked
Yo he sido atacado

The broke into my apartment
Robado mi apartamento

They stole my wallet
Se robaron mi billetera

I want to report a crime
Quiero reportar un crimen

I want to file a police report
Quiero presentar un informe de la policía

I need to contact my embassy
Necesito contacto con mi embajada

I want to speak with a lawyer
Quiero hablar con un abogado

I lost my money
Perdí mi dinero

I forgot my passport
Se me olvidaba mi pasaporte

I left the keys in the room
Dejé las llaves en la habitación

I want to leave this place
Quiero dejar este lugar

Chapter 37

Taxi & Hiring a Car

I want to hire a car
Quiero aqluilar un coche

I need it for one week
Lo quiero para una semana

Please explain the documents
Por favor explicar los documentos

Must I return the car here?
¿Tengo que devolver el coche aquí?

Is there a charge per kilometre?
Se cobrar el kilometraje?

Please show me how to operate the car?
Por favor muéstrame como se manejan el coche

I would like to rent a small size car
Me gustaría alquilar un coche de tamaño pequeño

I would like to rent a large car
Me gustaría alquilar un coche grande

Do you have a car with automatic?
¿Tienes un coche con transmisión automática?

I want to leave the car at the airport
Quiero dejar el coche en el aeropuerto

Where is the tool kit?
Dónde está la caja de herramientas?

We don't need additional insurance!
No queremos seguro adicional!

What is the emergency number?
¿Cuál es el número de emergencia?

Where can I get a taxi?
¿Dónde puedo tomar un taxi?

Take me to the airport please
Lléveme al aeropuerto por favor

The bus station please
La estación de autobuses por favor

Take me to this address
Lléveme a esta dirección

Why is it so expensive
¿Por qué es tan caro?

Can you help me with the suitcase
¿Me puede ayudar con la maleta?

Please don't interrupt our conversation
Por favor no interrumpas nuestra conversación

Turn off the music please
Por favor apagar la música

Turn on the taxi meter
Encienda el taxímetro

Chapter 38

General Repairs

This is damaged
Esto está dañado

This is broken
Esto está roto

Can you repair it?
¿Puede repararlo?

Can you do it quickly?
¿Puede hacerlo rápidamente?

What's the problem?
¿Cuál es el problema?

Can you get a spare part?
¿Se puede obtener una pieza de repuesto?

Can you glue it?
¿Pegarla? / Puedes pegarlo?

Here is the guarantee
Aquí es la garantía

Can you take a look at it?
Puede mirar esto?

We need help here
Nosotros necesitamos ayuda aquí

We need a specialist
Necesitamos un especialista

We need a replacement
Necesitamos un reemplazo

I need nails and a hammer
Necesito clavos y un martillo

I need a saw
Necesito una sierra

Who can fix it?
¿Quién la puede arreglar?

Chapter 39

Going to Church

We are protestants
Somos protestantes

We are catholic
Somos católicos

We are muslims
Somos musulmanes

We are buddhists
Somos budistas

Do you believe in God?
¿Cree usted en Dios?

What is your religion
Cuál es su religión

We are very religious
Somos muy religiosas

We are not religious
No somos religiosos

We want to walk the Camino de Santiago
Queremos andar el Camino de Santiago

We go to church on Sundays
Vamos a la iglesia los domingos

At what time does the mass start?
¿A que hora comienza la misa?

Where is the synagogue?
¿Dónde está la sinagoga?

Where is the mosque?
¿Dónde está la mezquita?

I would like to see a priest
Me gustaría ver a un sacerdote

I would like to pray
Me gustaría orar

Let us pray together
Oremos juntos

Religious holiday
Fiesta religiosa

The bible is important to me
La Biblia es importante para mí

Is there a bible study group?
¿Hay un grupo de estudio bíblico?

Chapter 40

Seasons, Festivals and Public Holidays

the seasons
los tiempos

spring
Primavera

summer
Verano

autumn
Otoño

winter
Invierno

January
Enero

February
Febrero

March
Marzo

April
Abril

May
Mayo

June
Junio

July
Julio

August
Agosto

September
Setiembre

October
Octubre

November
Noviembre

December
diciembre

Chapter 41

Public Holidays

January 1, New Year's Day
Año Nuevo

Holy Thursday
Jueves Santo

Good Friday
Viernes Santo

May 1, Labour Day
Día del Trabajo

St. John's Day
Día de San Juan Bautista

January 6, Epiphany
Día de Reyes

Corpus Christi Day
Corpus Christi

15 August, Assumption
Asunción

12 October, Columbus Day
Día de Hispanidad

1 November, All saints Day
Todos los Santos

6 December, Constitution Day
Día de la Constitución

8 December, Immaculate Conception
Inmaculada concepción

24 December Holy Night
Noche de Paz

25 December, Christmas Day
Navidad

Chapter 42

Trivial Conversation Phrases

Where are you going?
¿A donde vas?

Are you here on holidays?
¿Estas aquí de vacaciones?

I would like to invite you
Me gustaría invitarle

I doesn't matter
No importa

We are just passing through
Nosotros estamos de paso

I can cook for you
Yo puedo cocinar para usted (ti)

It will be good
Va a ser bien

Do you know..?
¿Sabes..?

I can help you
Te puedo ayudar

I am good at it
Soy bueno con este

I need a protection suntan cream
Necesito una crema de bronceado de protección

What is your favorite color?
¿Cuál es tu color favorito?

come / come along
Ven

Can I join you?
¿Puedo acompañarlo?

Please wait here
Por favor espere aquí

This is forbidden!
¡Esto es prohibido!

Can I smoke here?
¿Puedo fumar aquí?

Do you have a question?
Tienes una pregunta?

Do you mind if I..?
¿Te molesta si yo.?

Let's do it together!
Vamos a hacerlo juntos! / Hacemos juntos!

Let's celebrate!
Vamos a celebrar!

Chapter 43

Signs and Notices

open
abierto

closed
cerrado

hot
caliente / calor

cold
frio

beautiful
hermoso / bonito

ugly
feo

empty
vacio

full
lleno

new
nuevo

old
viejo

clean
limpia

dirty
sucio

bright
Brillante

dark
oscuro

cheap
barato

expensive
caro

interesting
interesante

boring
aburrido

friendly
agradable

unfriendly
hostil

nice / pleasant
amable

a great time
un tiempo estupendo

lucky
suerte

bad luck
mala suerte

generous
generosa

stingy
tacaños

honest
honesta

dishonest
deshonesto

free
libre / gratuita

for sale
se vende

to rent
se aquilar

I agree
De acuerdo

Chapter 44

Legal Terms & Words

the deed
la escritura

A contract
un contrato

an agreement
un acuerdo

We need to sign the....
Tenemos que firmar el....

It's already confirmed
Ya está confirmado

the lawyer / attorney
el / la abogado(a)

the judge
el juez

to denounce
para denunciar

criminal charges
cargos criminales

to bail someone
para rescatar a alguien

You are accused of...
se le acusa de...

a trial
un ensayo / tribunal

I have to go to court
Tengo que ir a un tribunal

lawyer's fee
honorario de abogado

state attorney
abogado de estado

extradition to another country
extradición a otro país

Do I have to pay a fine?
¿Tengo que pagar una multa?

Are we protected by bankruptcy law¿
¿Estamos protegidos por la ley de quiebra?

Is our business against labor laws?
¿Es nuestro negocio contra el derechos laborales?

What are the legal requirements?
¿Cuáles son los requisitos legales?

We would like to register our....
Nos gustaría registrar nuestro....

What is my legal status?
¿Cuál es mi situación legal?

Who has custody?
Quien tiene la custodia?

I am not guilty
Yo no soy culpable

I will sue you for fraud
Va demandar por fraude

NOTES

One of the best ways to learn Spanish fast is reading Spanish short stories for beginners. This book will enhance your reading skills, improve your vocabulary and entertain you with captivating stories. You will also discover many anecdotes of Spanish cultures and customs. This book includes audio and paragraph-by-paragraph translations, a truly bilingual story and textbook that will help you in many ways, now available on all major book platforms.

www.ingramcontent.com/pod-product-compliance
Lightning Source LLC
Chambersburg PA
CBHW042116100526
44587CB00025B/4079